The Hidden Source

Richard Rose

Copyright© 2023 Richard Rose
ISBN: 978-81-19228-65-2

First Edition: 2023
Rs. 200/-

Cyberwit.net
HIG 45 Kaushambi Kunj, Kalindipuram
Allahabad - 211011 (U.P.) India
http://www.cyberwit.net
Tel: +(91) 9415091004
E-mail: info@cyberwit.net

Printed at Replika Press Pvt. Ltd.

"Poetry is written by blind men groping in the dark."

Brendan Kennelly

The title of this collection comes from Derek Mahon's poem "Everything is Going to be All Right."

The lines flow from the hand unbidden

And the hidden source is the watchful heart;

The sun rises in spite of everything,

And the far cities are beautiful and bright.

Observations on Richard Rose's published works

Richard Rose's short story collection, *The Artist's Model and Other Stories,* takes readers on an unforgettable journey. In stately, elegant prose, he offers up a parade of life's little secrets. Time stops and starts as these stories twist and turn, and his characters find strange hints from the past that by the end turn out to be true. It's a haunting journey, with a surprise on every page.

Martin Golan, Author of the novels *"One Night with Lilith"* and *"My Wife's Last Lover"*

The Artist's Model and Other Stories is aimed at the thoughtful reader, the person who turns things over in his or her mind and delights in the discovery of each new skin of the literary onion. It is an immense pleasure to be led through an intellectual landscape by a guide so competent, assured, and unobtrusive that you forget he is there and imagine that the power of the reaction you experience is the product of your own perspicacity. An object lesson in what the short story or good fiction of any format or genre is supposed to do.

David Gardiner author of the novel *"Engineering Paradise"*

In this moving collection, (*The Artist's Model and Other Stories*) Richard Rose touches on various topics such as travel, nature, art, and music. Whatever he writes about, he always demonstrates a deep knowledge of the subject and a subtle understanding of psychology and the human condition. He skilfully builds a narrative, keeping the reader in suspense until the very end. But at the end of the story, he does not attempt to strike the reader's imagination with some unexpected surprises, but rather seeks to reassure the reader that, despite suffering and failure, there is beauty in the world and goodness in the human heart.

Boris Kokotov author of *Welcome to the Smashing Center.*

Letters to Lucia is funny, thought provoking, erudite and entertaining, in equal measure. But above all it is poignant — the outline of Lucia's tragic life is laid bare, alongside her illustrious father's attempts to cope with it.

Irish Post

For Joyce enthusiasts and those who would like to know more about this extraordinary family and its links to Dublin, Paris, Zurich, Trieste and Northampton, *"Letters to Lucia"* represents a valuable addition to existing Joycean commentary from a unique angle.

Senator David Norris, James Joyce scholar and member of the Oireachtas, Ireland

Rose writes with beautiful imagery. Each story (*Breaching the Barriers: Stories and Essays from India*), perfectly captures the feel, the place, the voice of the tale being told and the characters in them.

LB Sedlacek author of *"The Poet Next Door,"* and *"The Jackalope Committee and Other Short Stories."*

Contents

Homecoming

Absence,
necessary often, but seldom welcomed.
Distance between us sometimes great,
but always measured in mere milage,
never through a lessening affection.
And as days pass contact is maintained
no matter what the cost or challenges
of time zones, or fallible systems of communication.
The return, eagerly anticipated,
as days and hours counted down to zero
pass slowly, but with expectation ever heightened.
Ah, then at last the homecoming.
Ecstasy,
soft lips on warm familiar flesh.

Return to Gower

(for Sara)

Looking from the picture window,
across Rhossili's churchyard stones,
lichen-bloomed amongst the skittish grasses.
Out beyond a breeze-blessed shimmered sea,
fringed with cream and curling foam,
that washed away the vows of lovers,
just lately etched in sand.
The sifting morning sunlight
awakes the hunch-backed slopes of Bury Holms.
This sacred place first visited,
almost fifty years before,
where some things long since changed,
and others so familiar are the same.
And down through all these years,
you have remained constant.

"Death Cannot Steal the Light"

Memorial to the poet Vernon Watkins, St Mary's Church Pennard

Two women arranging flowers when we came into the church,
a wedding at midday they say, three hours yet,
please do come in.
The memorial, a neat plaque, black with lettering in gold,
a name, dates, and final words from 'Great Lines Returning'.
A commemoration understated, much as you had lived your life,
softer than your revered Swansea friend, and sadly less remembered.
Nothing much to see here, is what many might have told us.
True enough, but I was glad we came to pay respects,
to one whose words I'd read, that moved me so,
those many years ago.

Porpoise

Two seconds then gone,
then two seconds more.
Scything dorsal fin
and sleek black hump of back.
Two more precious seconds,
then gone again.
The sightings momentary,
but still they bring to us
a quickening of the pulse.
Two seconds of privilege,
then two seconds more,
then gone.

Thurlestone Plovers

Rich pickings amongst wrack and kelp,
that slides and shifts on lapping tide,
for ring-necked plovers that dash and turn,
with blurring strides and watchful gaze.
Always alert to those roguish gulls,
that swooping low with ill-intent,
act the bully-boy to claim the ground,
to scatter the waders and force a flight.
Now gathered once more along the strand,
the plovers will recommence their hunt,
to scavage beneath the bronzy fronds,
until the airborne thugs return.
And thus disturbed, a ritual repeated,
of skimming above the curling waves,
swift across the rock-split foam,
that lashes crags at Thurlestone Arch.
For now, they'll seek to graze in peace,
to prod the sands and strut their dances,
but know that to settle for long is no option,
and so is defined their cycle of days.

Fieldfares

An angry northern wind claws flesh
and reddened leaves of hawthorn scatter driven,
tumbling on the blasted late November air.
Booted feet skate insecure on mudded tracks,
heads bowed, observant, mindful of the need
for care with each step taken down the slope.

Chatterings of fieldfares chase in ragged clusters,
create distorted shapes, defined then redefined.
Twisting dark funambulists skirting over hedges,
black ragged outlines picked out against a slated sky.
Here comes at last a longed-for entertainment,
in recent weeks these birds not yet arrived but
eagerly awaited, to bring relief on dismal days,
souvenirs of warmth against the bitter months ahead.

Indistinct horizons, confused abstract shaped outlines,
maybe hills, perhaps the tangled heads of forest trees.
These sunless, hoary days conspire to steal the vista
remarked spectacular, when last we'd made this summit.
A month ago or less, we might with greater confidence
have named those veiled places that we now surmise.
At this, the dog-end of the year, the warming hours
of autumn, relegated to our memories are mourned.

As bones grow older, chills run deep and winter days,
that once were greeted with a shrug are now accepted
grudgingly, and pulling collars high around our necks
we look again for acrobatic flights of birds to brighten days,
and keep us ever hopeful, as antidote against the looming grey.

A man who talks to trees

Of late, while walking in the woods,
I've seen a man who talks to trees.
His words are softly spoken, tender,
though I sense some sorrow as he speaks.
I saw him there again today,
while taking care he'd not see me,
anxious that I may disturb
a conversation made in privacy.
And then from out of silence,
I thought I heard the trees reply.
A murmur indistinct, or maybe just
a zephyr whispering through the leaves.
Before he left the scene, this stranger,
a man who knows the languages of trees,
gently stroked rough bark of oak,
and as he parted I could see
the sadness written on his face,
as might be seen in he who mourns
the loss of one much loved.

Lapwings

There was a time not long ago,
I'd not have deemed it worthy
to comment as I did today,
on acrobatic flights of lapwings,
silhouetted black and white
against a pristine sky.

Those were days when often viewed,
above the fields around our home,
not long after the harvest time,
those pirouetting graceful birds,
would weave cavorting shapes,
and brighten winter days.

But here today above still waters,
we rejoiced, a flock of thirty seen,
or maybe more, whose elegant caprice,
caused us both to stand a while,
and trace their paths across the sky,
a sight that made us glad.

I like to think that there's a chance,
that there will come a time once more,
when from my study window,
I'll look out over frosted fields
where lapwings may be seen again
to grace our local skies.

Stonechat

Truly a narcissist.
There at the topmost spike of gorse,
with stately bearing, bill jutting,
beneath a sooty crown,
fringed by a priestly collar.
How well you know your finest feature,
that russet breast all puffed out proud.
Turning about you check to see,
that your audience of great admirers
are giving due reverence to your show.
Count me amongst their number.

Soon Leaving

Yesterday there were just six,
close gathered on the wire.
This morning's count was twenty-two,
and had I hung around a little longer,
the congregation would have been still greater.
For days now, these welcome summer residents
with nature's intuition, have responded to the signs,
the shortening days, the softening light,
the drawing in and cooling of the evenings.
Far fewer now for them those frantic insects
that had pranced above the glinting river's surface,
a bounteous harvest feasted on all summer.
And so, I know that southern climes must beckon,
and should I pass this way next week, those
swallows that have graced our skies,
to court us with their lithesome prance,
will then, most likely have departed.

Seasons

The tousled forest lifts its head, and sings
to a minacious, ashen sky, as rusted leaves
spin and pirouette their airy path to earth,
in percussion pianissimo, accompaniment
to a gentle lilt of softly murmured breeze.

The timbre of this autumn lyric, golden rich and deep,
far distanced from the virgin notes of springtime,
before those novice voices had matured and been
rehearsed, across fast dwindling hazy summer days.

Today the earthy tones I hear rebounding,
surpass those heard when in days not long past,
birdsong held the top-line and confined the trees
subservient, in a canopy of lilting chorus lines.

With the coming of the cold short days of winter,
the muffled forest voices soon must fade,
though even then they never will fall silent,
as they wait, for a new cycle to begin.

From early childhood we have learned this pattern,
of seasons, each distinguished by its rhythms,
that brings us reassurance, as it passes,
with melodies that chant regeneration.

And from this oft sung cycle we have learned,
to understand the cadence of our lives,
a sequence of rebirth across the ages,
where with the seasons we must grow then pass,
but in doing so we know the song goes on.

Ladies in Waiting

Ladies in waiting,
one hundred or more,
lying beneath the blasted ridge.
Hard against hedges,
crouching for shelter,
they turned powdered faces,
to watch us pass by.

Early this morning, low in the valley
lambs, though not new-born,
a month or more aged.
Alarmed at our coming,
skipped to protection,
summoned by ewes.
The sisters of those,
the ladies in waiting.

High on the hillside
those ladies in waiting,
tearing at tussocks and
biding their time.
Gathering strength,
awaiting their moment,
until they no longer
will be ladies in waiting.

Winter Dawn

Charcoal night fades
as the chiaroscuro hour
alarums the coming dawn,
revealing a silhouette of trees.
A watercolourist's palette
subtle pinks and mauves
smudge the stilling clouds
of brightening early sky.
Rising slowly from the earth,
the seeping blood of morning
quickens as strength intensifies.
Until beyond wooded horizon
as if consumed by flame,
the world is charged vermilion,
revealing fields of crystalline,
trees white-tressed with rime.
Winter morning bitter-sweet,
with biting air and glorious light,
when stamping feet against the cold
my warm breath forming clouds,
dissipates defeated by chill air.

The Fly Tippers

Futile I know when first I try to hide behind denial,
maintaining my gaze upwards to the skyline.
Here, where new mown fields of stubble,
burnished gold, kiss the clean empyrean blue,
I find assurance in the landscape that I favour.
Ravilious might have marked this land,
caught the drifting shadows of soft clouds,
captured light, fingering through dancing leaves.
And others too would celebrate the scene surveyed,
one familiar but renewed with every viewing,
comforting consistency a welcome feature.
Clare country, shaped over centuries by custodians,
who care with pride and nurture crops and livestock,
lay the hedges, mend the stiles and win the harvest,
their labours etched on every inch of this rich land.
Here where buzzards wheel and mew, and skylarks,
trilling well-rehearsed arpeggios and scales ascend,
to celebrate these long warm summer days.
This the English idyll, bucolic sure and timeless
that maybe after all, we take too much for granted.
Truth no longer to be denied reveals a cruel perspective,
challenging the promises that I had vowed to keep,
to walk along the pathways and drink sweet air of renewal,
to clear my mind and seek to find some ease from the day's toil.
Here, beside the very viewpoint that caused for celebration,
grim detritus stacked and spewing unwelcome across the lane.
An angry scar, a wounded hedgerow victim of assault,
an act of pre-planned violence by those who have no care,
no sense of honour or respect, no concept of such glories,

that had they paused only a moment might have been revealed.
I pity those who came last night under a veil of darkness,
oblivious to the landscape now despoiled by their actions,
those who came with one intent to jettison their rubbish.
I grieve for the soulless fly tippers who with contempt for beauty,
ignorant of the inheritance freely gifted through generations,
left me feeling angry, when I should have found great joy.

Tryfan, North Ridge

Pausing our efforts breathless above the Milestone,
resting just where the ill-shaped path had steepened,
where sedge and rush gave way to shifting stone,
and pipits called from rocks lost in the mist.
Quartz crystal there imprisoned in dark rhyolite,
beside the shifting screes and still cold peated-pools,
revealing treads of those who came before us,
signing the way where others yet would follow.
Jagged ridge vertebra above, forbidding, harsh and grey,
throw down the gauntlet as we seek to find the skyline,
where the ghosting mists whipped up and drifted,
to secrete the way, we sought to gain safe passage.
Route finding so we had heard, would not be easy,
and so it proved, causing us to doubt and question,
seeking for credence as hands on rock came in to play,
where close to towering cliffs we craned to find direction.
The rock proved good, the holds secure and comforting,
with footing sure as boots gripped firm and true.
Progress was slow, but confidence came as height was gained,
and affinity strengthened as we came to know the mountain.
Welcome sun breaks through the rising clouds, caressing limbs,
with warmth that comes with promises of rewards to be gained,
as pulling over steps and ledges we pause to view the scene,
of Carnedds towering over Ogwen, shrugging shoulders under clouds.
But then, as was its right to do, the crag enforced authority,
commanding us to know our place, lest we should grow complacent,
to remind us of the mountain's due of homage and respect,
as now we found ourselves beneath a cliff that would not yield.
Off course for sure, the way before us barred by louring faces,

that frowned and scowled and forced us to accept we must retreat,
to retrace not without hazard, precarious steps just scaled,
to search again for easier ground to re-join once more the ridge.
On firmer ground we stood beneath a gully broad, forbidding,
wherein wedged boulders might with care and wit be overcome,
and so, we thrutched, and heaved in hope of firmer ground above,
knowing that such venture would mean no going back.
The steepening crest now won at last, brought our objective nearer,
as efforts eased and with confidence, we climbed the final tower,
to reach the summit where we knew we'd find the famous landmark,
Adam and Eve, twin monoliths set firm on gritted ground.
And all around majestic purple peaks and ridges shone,
Glyders, Carnedds and cold slated Ogwen in the valley,
to hold our gaze until descending screes that paved the way,
past Idwal Lake and Bochlwyd and rough tufted green below.
Such mountain days will make for long-lived memories,
and those that lodge most fondly in my mind,
were all hard won and gained in favoured company,
each step made upon the ridge assured a day worthwhile.

Farne Islands

The boatman, reading runes of foaming eddies,
a lore long mastered now his constant guide,
brought us to those spume lashed ledges,
where churn and lurch of open waters,
eased in the lee of the high cliff side.

Craning to see broad stepped walls above us,
where dark rock, guano splashed and crusted,
cracked and jutted like an old crone's tooth.
Ten thousand seabirds claimed possession,
clung tight to the ledges with no space wasted.

Our presence announced by kittiwake fanfares,
heralding the onset of a chorus of calls,
brown headed guillemots shuffling position,
sharp-eyed razorbills each vying for space,
and there on the skyline a dancing of gulls.

Skimming low above deep roiling waters,
with furious wingbeats the puffins appear,
rainbow bills well laden with sand eels,
seeking safe landing they rise up on the draught,
twisting and tumbling their dance in the air.

The Farnes for now provide a safe haven,
craggy refuge lashed by cold North Sea tides,
nature still maintains a tenuous hold,
while elsewhere her grip fast slips away,
leaving the weakest with nowhere to hide.

Might it be that this glorious spectacle,
that my generation is privileged to know,
may soon be confined to the pages of textbooks,
that cause us to mourn for wonders now lost,
through our indifference, and actions too slow?

Will my grandchildren visit these islands,
bringing their children to see what I've seen?
Will they make journeys to witness the wonders,
that long we'd assumed would be here forever?
Or will this become a sad distant dream?

If guillemots follow the fate of the dodo,
and memories of razorbills begin to fade.
If puffins confined to the pages of picture books
disappear from our landscape, then we shall rue
the pathetic inadequacy of decisions we made.

Working the Locks

The crank of rachet against greasy pawl.
chattering and grating as the windlass turns,
and rushing waters gush from open paddles,
to roar and slap against the brick lock sides.
Gates creak and groan as taken by the water,
they slowly shift until finally freed,
and straining our efforts against the balance beam,
they are pushed open wide for passage to proceed.
Release the rattling paddles and return heavy gates,
to rest again as barriers against the weighty surge.
Repeat at Tardebigge, times by thirty.
Repeat at Hatton, times by twenty-one.
Descend Caen Hill with effort, times by twenty-nine.
From Gayton to Northampton, times by seventeen.

Burial of the King at Sutton Hoo

Eorpwald, son of the great warrior king,
summoned all who swore allegiance to attend.
And so they came, each one to pay tribute,
fine noblemen and humble kinsmen all.
On foot and horseback, crossing gorsey heath,
through oaken shaded forest tracks they came.
With sail and oar, old men, brothers, sons
along the mud churned Deben waters came.
From Gipeswic town and every village round,
from the wind scoured Anglian shore, they came.
Every man knew his duty, to do full honour,
to laud their mighty leader and so they came.
In numbers beyond counting, how they came,
be sure today they came, be sure they came.
And it was good to see how many came.

Raedwald son of Tytila, brother of Eni,
though greater far for sure than both of these.
He who slew the mighty Aethelfrith,
in bloody conflict beside the banks of Idle.
None his equal in the sweat of battle,
many feared the vengeance of his hefty axe.
No man ever could have seen him yield,
when age alone would prove to be his equal.
Time has come to offer homage to the king,
not one man doubted that today he'd come.
And it was right today so many came,
and it was good to see how many came.

Stately clothed in finest kingly vestments,
there displayed upon the richest furs.
Gold and garnet clasped his royal cloak,
his helmet shield and armour by his side.
See how even brave men stare and tremble,
at that axe that cleaved both flesh and bone,
that split the skull of fearful Aethelfrith,
and sent him screaming early to his grave.
With bowed heads each man pays a silent tribute,
a supplication to their once great leader.
And as they passed each man was glad he came,
all knew that it was only right they came.

The ship well-furnished for the great departing,
to ensure Raedwald's comfort on his journey.
Fine plates and bowls of silver were provided,
with cups of horn and bowls of polished maple.
And neither would he want for entertainment,
with gaming pieces and a lyre to give sweet music.
Green oak timbers riveted with iron,
secured the vessel for the king's last mission.
When all had been inspected and approved,
the loyal subjects left the scene behind them.
But each man said that he was glad he came.
Evermore to be told, that day when many came.

My Grandfather's Allotment

(Nathaniel Charles Terrett 1905 - 1994)

My grandfather had an affinity with soil,
he read it every bit as well as I might read a book.
Heavy clay weighed upon his rust-hobbed boots,
along with loam beneath his graft-chipped fingernails,
these features marked for me his manly signature.
Flat cap, scuff-sleeved old tweed jacket, shirt
open at the neck, best forgotten old grey trousers,
held up with a cracked black leather belt,
this the uniform by which he would be always recognised.
The allotment patch comfortable in its familiarity,
neat but never to the point of obsession, indulged
with loving care like that he lavished on his family.
This hallowed place, of little consequence to others,
but where he, more at home than when at home, found
space for solitary contemplation as he turned each sod.
I see him at those moments of his great contentment,
whistling and tilling his way through the evening's toil,
and remember the pride with which, at the end of labours,
old canvas bicycle bags bore witness rich and heavy,
well laden with the bounty of his manly hours of effort.
Just reward he'd have said, not for his work alone,
but rather for the pact he made long days since with the earth,
that sacred ground at which, if work is truly worship,
he had long been its most respectful supplicant.
But I knew only too well that when the time should come,
and decisions made would steal from him the narrow
strip of land, in which he long invested so much love,

that then his final parting would not be so far behind.
And so it was, and to this day I wonder at that act of treachery.
But I will remember always, a man at one with the soil,
that served him well and brought him many gifts,
in gratitude for the care he tendered over many years.

A Fading Shadow

A fading shadow curled and twisted on the bed,
though never still, twitching just enough to show
that life of sorts, though now a struggle, still remains.
A shadow, a darkened silhouette and hardly more than that.
The character of earlier days we look for, now long stolen,
vitality once recognised and loved, absent themselves.
We know now of a cruel zone, a time of wracked confusion,
a space conflicted between what we once had known as life,
that is now mere existence beyond all comprehension.
Unfathomable despair defies all efforts made to understand,
those emotions that even now appear to fill your troubled mind,
those thoughts locked in to emphasise our own pathetic efforts.
And just as shadows disappear once the evening sun goes down,
your senses fade away and memories must descend still further,
and through deepening confusion you must be forever lost.

Final meeting

I cannot call to memory the last time we held hands.
In infancy it would have been, because you taught me early,
that actions such as these were not seemly among men.

Displays of overt affection never really were your style,
though occasions I recall when your mask slipped just enough
to reveal beneath your carapace a far more gentle soul.

A kindly nurse prepared me before she let me in, to sit
upon the chair, squeezed in beside your bed, in which I knew,
that this would be the last where you would lay and find some rest.

Your hearing, she informed me, would be the last sense to depart,
and I was glad there might be time, and as I bent to whisper,
hoped that you might hear words that should not be left unsaid.

Looking down I saw your frail hand, limp lying on white sheets,
and taking hold I knew this time the choice was mine alone,
and sensed you'd not refuse me now, even had you been able.

No place remained for manly postures in those final hours,
when this most simple contact brought late comfort to us both,
when we held hands just as we might have sixty years ago.

I feel you gently squeeze my hand and take this as affirmation,
a reminder of what we both have lost when all goodbyes are said,
and once again I wonder when we might have last held hands.

House clearance

Must this be the drawing of a line?

A life of experiences shrouded beneath dust.
This once upon a time,
this long-loved home
now condemned to silence.

All must return unto dust.

Alone, all souls departed, a hollow shell remains.
Artefacts, those souvenirs of life,
some once treasured,
others mere necessities.

Discarded to the skip of oblivion.

With each black plastic sack removed,
another decade fades.
One final twist of key in a lock,
I lower my eyes to the threshold,

Once so familiar, but soon to be no longer crossed.

Blind Faith

There have been times when I could almost envy
those whose faith, though blind may see them through.
The certainty that belief instils through knowing,
that all the preacher tells them must be true.
Then reason gives me every cause to doubt,
and justify assertions made with words,
so readily transported from the pulpit
to sugar-coat the bitter pills of life.
When certitude bruised by interrogation,
challenges the hegemonic stream,
then must the restless mind cast shadows,
where others stand content to live the dream.
I have no cause to chide those who find comfort,
in words passed to them through the generations.
Each one must strive to find his own salvation,
for some contentment comes with veneration.
I too once walked along a narrow pathway,
that those my betters, told me led to freedom.
But I grew worldly-wise and saw around me,
how doctrine unchallenged leads to devastation.
A troubled mind creates a state agnostic,
where all that once held true is called to question.
This preferred to a life which unexamined,
may shatter dreams if all proves an illusion.

Graham*

Yours a life of service,
played out not within the glare of spotlights,
but rather treading softly through darkened paths,
along the rugged byways where others hesitate to go,
unassuming, shunning acclamation.
Philosophy nowhere written or recorded,
but evidenced through commitment shaped by action,
strong in your beliefs, purposeful and honest,
with each endeavour made to leave this world
a gentler place than when you had first found it.
How many felt the blessings of your mission?
those who others chose to disregard,
when you with firm resolve ignored the doubters,
and sought to understand the troubled lives,
of others whose days are lived out on the margins.
While many seek rewards or affirmation,
you knew that medals quickly lose their gloss,
but I hope you gained deserved satisfaction,
in seeing how each act of kindness wrought,
showed that we might build a better future,
one in which all may take their rightful place.
Were you here today to hear others laud your virtues,
you would have sought the shadows to avoid their gaze.
Self-conscious, understated and yes, perhaps even fearful,
never sure that what you did was quite enough,
anxious that the vision that you held might not be shared,
knowing that so many others had given up or doubted.
But those of us whose privilege was to know you,
who witnessed the compassion that drove each action taken,

know that we along with far too many unnamed others,
are indebted to a man whose life was truly lived through service.

*Graham Matthews was a friend and colleague who devoted his
life to the service of others. This poem was written for him and
more especially for his wife Denise and the many friends who
mourn his passing. It was read at his memorial service.

"All the Men and Women Merely Players"

Age enters silent as a haar,
inveigling slowly over salt washed sands,
chilling bones, stiffening joints,
dulling every wit with cruel North Sea air.

Walking on broad wind braced strands,
shoulders stooped, body leant against a wall of wind,
senses awakened by suck and blow of tide,
with shrill gulls screaming against a pewter sky.
This is what it means to be alive.
This the moment, here and now, never to be recaptured.
Feel the seconds passing, listen for the heartbeat,
celebrate the sting of salt and harsh abrasive sand.
Here where nature's power and all her elements conspire,
to dwarf pathetic efforts of dissent,
to stop the clocks and hide behind those memories,
now mocking all those lies of times long lost,
when running free and careless we denied the fleeting time.

No regrets.
Nature's way demands that years roll on.
Just as tides and moons must wax and wane,
so must we all embrace the long set pattern,
to see it otherwise would be obtuse.
Each of the bard's seven ages brings its blessings,
each its tribulations, each its mysteries and riddles.
Who would want it any other way?
Not I for sure

Pitmen Painters

I

Today we were the only ones who wandered,
treading quietly as may aptly have befitted a chapel.
Were we affording some due reverence that caused us
to speak infrequently, and then only in hushed tones?
Respect most certainly, admiration without doubt,
and for my own part, although I had known these images,
reproduced a hundred times on pages and on screen,
an element of awe, far greater than expected, stilled me.
No artifice in these pictures hung around the walls,
nothing contrived, only the lived experiences of men,
those who knew and understood the reality here shown,
the labours and the joys of days with comrades and with family.
The grimy black and gritted truth of days beneath the earth,
this captured, yes, though never to provoke our sympathy,
or to depict the undisputed harshness of their sweated toil,
but set alongside images of family, of leisure, and of love.
Pitmen Painters a sobriquet allotted to these noble men,
a label of convenience, perhaps to narrow focus,
maybe a distraction from the true meaning of these works.
For here surely what we see today arrayed around these walls,
is the story of community as told by men who have earned the right,
to be respected as the artists who gave us their own Ashington.

II
Robert Lyon (1894 – 1978)
First Among Equals

Good intentions turned about.
In Ashington the vision held was swept away,
yielding to another yet far nobler.
Hearing the voices of men whose sharp intellect,
possibly far greater than even you had realised,
enabled you to show yourself a trusted leader.
Standing at the helm, you gently steered the boat,
with only the lightest touch upon the rudder.
Every member of the crew acknowledging authority,
could feel the way in which you coaxed them forward.
Today the reverence afforded you in Ashington,
well-deserved through personal ambition set aside,
enabling those who had indeed helped to shape a vision,
to gain the acclamation that they each receive today.

III
A Boy's Day – Oliver Kilbourn (c1938)

Woken gently by candlelight.
Mother knows the truth that lies ahead,
watching him depart she remains unreconciled,
with thoughts still doubting that boy has become man.
How fearful must that first descent have been?
Did the clatter of the cage, the journey into darkness,
the heat and sooted air cause him to contemplate,
that this would be the pattern of a lifetime?
No longer the boy of yesterday,

today he laughs and banters with the rest,
concealing apprehensions like every man around him.
On returning home, seated at the table,
before the hearth his mother seeks assurance.
Such attention maybe welcomed, though he hesitates
to show, lest it may betray his entry into manhood.
Initiated into ways of men who crack the rock,
who haul the loads and share a manly joke at bait time,
the boy-man will for sure sleep easily tonight.
A body in transition must be quick to restore strength,
in preparation for this his new lifelong regime.

IV

Leslie Brownrigg
The Miner (1935)

Feel the heat, taste the dust,
and curse the roof that snags each vertebra,
one more scar, never to be noticed.
Biceps beyond aching,
hamstrings taut and shoulders heavy,
eyes stung, assaulted, reddened.
Both nostrils clogged, and ears ringing,
knuckles scraped raw against rock.
This once accursed labour now accepted,
as this fine man renews familiarity
with the hardened coalface every day.

V

George Blessed Whippets (c1939)

Two dogs to be set against each other in the race,
but not just yet.
Still, silent, focused.
Time today owned by no one but these men,
content to breathe clean air.
Still, silent, focused.
Feel the dogs straining for release,
they too relish the freedom of the day.
Still, silent, focused.
Men and dogs together off the leash,
these the hours they may call their own.
Still, silent, focused.
Away now, see them go!

VI

Arthur Whinnon Pit Incident (c1936)

News travels quickly through the streets,
Hermes with winged sandals brings the word,
and when he comes, he seldom bears glad tidings.
Gathered near the pit head with collective grief,
some shed tears of anguish, others of relief,
no not this time thank God, not one of mine.
Stooped men bear the burden of the stretcher,
a precious cargo, still and lifeless lies,
beneath rough cloth that fails to hide the truth.
Dark and sombre ochre are the colours,
dark and sombre captures the emotions.

These scenes etched deep on every mind,
of those who know, this will not be the last time.
Pray Thanatos sends not Hermes with his call,
please let this scene of sorrows pass me by.

VII
Fred Laidler Open Drawer (1950s)

Each tool has its place,
easily to hand, positioned as before.
These the implements of the craftsman,
mark his trade, signify his unique skills.
Spokeshave, drill and chisel,
each await their turn,
when decisions will be made, just so,
and the carpenter may demonstrate his learning.

VIII
Photograph
Outside the National Gallery (1948)

London by train to pay homage to the greats.
Ashington seems remote from here,
far closer now those Florentine piazzas,
far nearer the boulevards of Paris and of Rome.

Say it with Flowers

Sad Ophelia.
Madness fast on the heels of grief and love,
taints her mind and casts her to the shadows,
that lengthen as the sun that filled her heart,
falls beneath a darkening horizon.
How now may she at last convey her meaning,
to those who stood and watched her as she fell?
A brother who in helplessness can only gaze
and seek to cast the blame upon a prince.
He too possessed by bitter grief and anguish,
sees nothing through the veil that clouds his eyes.
A maid naïve, once beautiful and filled with joy,
had failed to find the words to speak of losses,
until she recollects the language of the flowers,
and with this lachrymose devise voices her adieu.
Here's woody sprigs of rosemary for remembrance,
here's bitter rue that hopes to bring some grace,
sweet fennel bound around with twisted columbines,
pansies for thought and daisies of bright face.
But never more can there again be violets,
all withered since Polonious was taken.
Ophelia knows only the language of the flowers,
beyond this all that will remain is silence.

Malvolio

I find myself conflicted.
Malvolio, a villain sure as any,
arrogance his metier,
pomposity his craft.
Intent to rise and leave behind
the motley hoi polloi, who he
deems to be beneath him.
Sniping with a razor tongue,
driven on by avarice and greed,
Olivia's steward uncompromising,
in casting others from his path
for elevation, status, wealth.
But now he's gone too far,
Maria soon will bring him down,
and gathers co-conspirators,
as Sir Toby marks his card,
they'll push him from his perch.
Destined to be ridiculed,
cross-gartered and with rictus grin,
prancing in yellow stockings,
he plays the fop and so their sport
of mischief must begin.
Imprisoned in a dungeon,
where no light may penetrate,
mocked now by a man called fool,
who proves much wiser than himself.
Yet in the end, when all's revealed,

I'm unsure how I feel.
Humiliated and brought low,
Malvolio has his just desserts.
But maybe matters went too far,
for now, we see a broken man.
Imperiousness has given way,
but in its place is cruelty,
which may be little better,
as victims have turned tables.
One form of inhumanity
superseded by another.
And now I fear that maybe,
Malvolio as he threatened,
may seek his sweet revenge
on the entire pack of players.

The Barren House

I stayed in a house that had no books,
each day I was there I aged six months.
On departure I made sure to note the address,
I needed to ensure I would not return.

Blue Plaque, Oxford

By chance I came upon the plaque,
set high upon a dressed stone post.
An inscription I thought aptly phrased,
three simple words summed up the man,
'historian of ideas', but so much more.

With time to spare, I stood a while,
recalling the little I had learned.
My limited reading of his works,
that had yet left their mark on me,
his profound sense of reality.

The proper study of mankind,
through which with great humility
he guided us to understand,
his two concepts of liberty,
to show how man could be set free.

At the Fontanka in Leningrad,
a tryst with Akhmatova made
has passed from history to lore.
A nightlong conversation shared,
summoning their youthful days.

Berlin forever to be known,
a 'Guest from the Future' immortalised,
for having called to say farewell
to a Russian poet who read to him
of heroes lost and humanity gained.

A quiet street in Headington,
where I had unexpectedly,
come by chance upon a plaque.
A simple token none-the less
gave cause for me to smile today.

Goodrich Castle

Strutting jackdaws, coal black eyed
reside today, where nobility once ruled.
Throned superior upon the lofty towers,
they lord it over green lands that surround.
While summer martins now command the air,
scooping low, then soaring to the heights,
their captive prey delivered up to eager bills,
of chicks impatient calling from the nests.

Shattered walls once hung with silk brocade,
and handsome tapestries depicting scenes bucolic,
beneath which ladies adorned in their finery
gave orders to a hundred scurrying minions.
Today these scenes give way to eerie silence,
but still the ghosts of yesterday are here,
as silently they glide along each corridor,
their haughty presence still pervades the air.

In times long passed, Strongbow at the ramparts,
ordered and commanded all that he surveyed,
his fiefdom passed through countless generations,
to those who surely felt themselves secure.
But history throughout the years has taught us,
that empires fade when built upon the sands,
that falsely present a façade of the mighty,
only to cede when subjected to time's siege.

For centuries the Goodrich walls had crumbled,
an ivy-strangled ruin at the skyline,

Wordsworth's noblest ruin in all Hereford,
sentinel above the Wye's meanders.
Today the castle stands, a proud reminder,
of days that signified a glorious past,
preserved so all who come here now may wonder,
at stories that have helped to shape a nation

Bellapais

Hunched beneath the scrubby slopes of hills
that tumble to Kyrenia and the sea,
walls give back the glow of midday sun,
and lizards raise their heads in praise of heat.
Seeking peace along the gold stoned corridors,
sheltered and cooled by kind Etesian winds,
as many others must have often done before,
we viewed a landscape wrapped now in tranquillity.
This place afforded sanctuary through centuries,
to those who fleeing new fallen Jerusalem
escaping Saladin's triumphant forces,
and others who had come to find a place
of solitude closed off from earthly matters.
Close by in a house, white walled, that stands
along a sloping street above the abbey,
Durrell once lived and stood as witness,
as madness possessed the island that he loved,
where he had come to seek for some serenity.
Bitter Lemons, reads the yellow plaque upon the wall.
Bitter Lemons is the work he left us.
A meditation on an island paradise,
lost to Durrell, destined never to return.

"Pillar of Shame"

Under cover of darkness on December 23rd, 2021, men came like robbers in the night, to dismantle and remove the sculpture "Pillar of Shame," created by the Danish artist Jens Galschiøt to commemorate the lives of those murdered by the Chinese Government in the 1989 Tiananmen Square Massacre. The sculpture, largely unknown by much of the world, through the actions of the Chinese authorities was given wide publicity and thereby emphasised the tragedy of Tiananmen Square and the oppression of free speech inflicted upon Hong Kong citizens.

It is false hope in desperate men
that the destruction of art
may hide the truths of history.
How can men who wield such power
be so much more naïve,
than those who they would wish to see
forget those inconvenient facts?
Are such men so deluded?
No, more than that.
No more than that.

They came at night, with hammers, drills and saws,
secretive and stealthy, hidden behind plastic sheets.
Did these, the simple-minded operatives believe, that
concealed behind screens, their mission might be less revealed?
Had they hoped despite the constant din of drilling,
that those who heard would detect innocence?

An everyday activity, conducted beneath a darkened shroud,
Poorly disguised as maintenance, a routine undertaking.

> No, more than that.
>> No more than that.

As fearful men sleep uneasy in their Beijing beds,
their lackeys sent to do their bidding, sweat and toil,
knowing time is limited, their mission needs completion before dawn.
Those hours of darkness favoured everywhere by criminals are precious,
if the calumny is to be accomplished and escape to be achieved,
before those who persist and claim their right to freedom,
rise from their beds to find such chaos wrought.
Those who seek for liberty, honesty and truth,

> No, more than that.
>> No more than that.

Tiananmen 1989. See how Tank Man bravely stands alone.
An armoured column manned by those who know and fear,
that many from around the world are holding breath and watching.
Indecision dictates that this stand-off will continue,
only until the instant when the fretful feel it's time to move.
Tanks in line, 59 in number halted by a single man,
What goes through his mind no one can say.
Who is he, this defiant loner? Who knows? Who dare say his name?
His image known throughout the world a symbol of defiance.

> No, more than that.
>> No more than that!

Memorials to tyranny are found around the globe,
until today Jens Galschiøt's sculpture passed by, quite unknown,
by all but those who seek to find and understand the story.
A "Pillar of Shame," aptly named reminder of the tragedy,

visited upon those who would give voice to thought,
and long to savour the tastes that come with freedom.
The destruction of a copper tower acknowledged now by millions,
shows the power of art to laugh at tyranny's oppression,
No, more than that.
So much more than that.

Can those who sit and tremble from behind closed doors,
conceive of such futility in their actions?
The desperate act conducted to exert control,
the efforts made in hopes to erase memory,
has served instead to bring attention to an audience,
far wider than there might have been had a choice been made,
to leave in place the art they came here to destroy,
the sculpture that has now been viewed by millions.
No, more than that.

Maybe many more than that.

Diaspora

Where are you from?
I hear the question often.
What I mean is,
where are you really from?
In a nation of mongrels who may know,
our origins or our birthright?

Fie-fih-foh-fum, what is the blood of an Englishman?

Did my forebears cross cold northern waters,
row their longships through the Anglian estuaries,
to build thatched houses on the eastern shoreline?
Perhaps the blood that courses through my veins,
the genes that set the pattern for my being,
were shaped within Rome's widening empire,
by men who came and built the roads,
whose very routes we follow to this day.
Might an early relative of mine have fought,
and shared the victory with William at Senlac Hill?
Along with men who brought new laws and took measure
of a nation to set the record straight in Domesday.
Early settlers all, who came and stayed
And shaped a nation, calling it their home.

Fie-fih-foh-fum, what is the blood of an Englishman?

Those men who left their homes to cross the Irish Sea,
who came to open wide the routes of navigation,
the waterways to carry goods from land to sea,

and laid the rails to join the nation's cities.
Welcomed for their labours, lauded for their industry,
despised for settling in the land they'd helped to build.
Still others, from each corner of an empire,
those lands from which this nation gained its wealth,
who came to work the mills and man the factories,
gifting to the country music, food and customs,
that today we celebrate and call our own.
Those men who fought and died beside my family,
proud to wear the colours of the king,
decorated, honoured and lauded for their courage,
but labelled for the colour of their skin.

Fie-fih-foh-fum, what is the blood of an Englishman?

Hadrian I hear them say, he had the right idea,
build a wall and make it strong, ensure it's high enough
to deter and repel those strange Barbarian hoards.
Man the barricades with sentries all along the way,
precautions badly needed to maintain our pedigree.
Reinforce our coastlines and keep a wary eye,
for those who come in little boats
and put our brave guards lives at risk
to sneak beneath the radar.
These foreigners should know their place,
and recognise for sure, no matter their situation,
they have no rights settle on our shore.

Fie-fih-foh-fum, what is the blood of an Englishman?

This land we seem so proud to call our home,
a place built on the sweat and blood of those who came,
to assist us in the shaping of a nation.

Those who came as free men to offer us their service,
and others brought in bondage to do their master's bidding.
Each one of these has left a mark, a fingerprint indelible,
wherever he has tilled the soil, or cut the cloth,
or pulled the levers, hewn the rock or pushed the buttons
that have turned the clogs and shaped a nation's destiny.
Which of us can know for sure the nature of our ancestry?
Ours a proud heritage, shaped by many cultures,
stirred within a melting pot that has made us what we are.

Fie-fih-foh-fum, what is the blood of an Englishman?

Where are you from?
I hear the question often.
What I mean is,
where are you really from?
In a nation of mongrels who may know,
our origins or our birthright?

Fie-fih-foh-fum, what is the blood of an Englishman?

Ghosts

There was a time I used to know them well,
those teeming streets I came to walk today.
Some still familiar, little changed from when
I hardly needed thought to find my way.
Of others here I am no longer sure.
Is this where stood the bookshop often browsed
in which I bought that paperback *Ulysses*?
A place of assignation with a hundred poets,
a beacon signalling treasures stored within.
If I should scan the bookshelves of my home today,
I'd surely find a dozen books I'd purchased here.
And even as I stand there on that once familiar street,
the glorious scent of paper and the textures of those spines,
as I run my hands along those shelves return to me.
How many others from this city might recall,
but hardly know it now clad in its current guise?
The window displays choices of a different kind,
some with extra cheese, with chillies or with ham.

Just around the corner in a small café,
a shilling in the juke box gave a choice of three
recent records that had made the "hit parade."
It must have been a Saturday as I recall, when
drinking muddy coffee from chipped cups,
the girl behind the counter shook her tresses just for me.
In an instant I was captured by her bidding smile.
With naivety of youth, I thought I'd made a hit,
only to find her laughing as my cheeks grew flushed,
and embarrassment acute left me gauche and tied my tongue,

and meant for sure that I would never return there.
Where now those long-lost days of childish innocence?
They too just like that café are confined to memory.

Northgate Street on route to Kingsholm Road,
I absent myself from school on a Wednesday afternoon,
choosing then to join a loud processing crowd,
as we made our way towards the hallowed rugby ground.
Speeches made, banners waved, slogans shouted loud,
to make our feelings known and to offer our support,
for those then singled out by the colour of their skin,
denied their right to be recognised and dignified,
or selected for a team named for their homeland.
I too had the privilege to play a game I loved,
on that ground where we protested on that day,
with friends who had walked those roads beside me,
and others who I knew would never have agreed.

Legend tells that Shakespeare had once visited.
A member of the King's Men to perform within the yard,
gazed down upon from balconies, harangued by bawdy crowds,
none would have known how he'd become revered.
Here within a bar discreetly squeezed into a corner,
with mates, like me all underage, trying to look the part,
supping ale from dimpled tankards, we'd put the world to rights,
just as others would have done four hundred years before.
Today the New Inn at first glance is much as I recall,
a friendly face though now possessed by strangers,
where I could once have entered through the archway,
assured I'd meet with pals who waited there to greet me.

Where might they be, all those I once knew well?
Companions of my early days within this place.

I sought them in the faces of many who passed by
but doubt that I would recognise them now.
Many, just like me would have moved away,
to seek for opportunities elsewhere.
It seems probable today that those who chose to stay
would have no reason to recall me well.
And yet around each corner as I walked today,
visiting old haunts that once had meaning,
I met the ghosts of yesterday within my mind,
that shape remembrance of now distant days.

No man has the power to halt the sands
as they run ever quicker through the timer.
And so, there is little point in looking back,
unless to do so aids us to remember,
days that have shaped and made us who we are,
times lost that can never be retrieved.
There are no ghosts save those that we imagine,
and even those we see today will fade from memory.

Glenn Gould Plays the Goldberg Variations

The puritans will cover their ears
and claim they seek authenticity.
Such a distraction they cannot abide,
must they be expected to tolerate
this intrusion upon sensibilities?
Johan Sebastian, they say for sure
would never approve such frivolity.
Though how they surmise this
with such bold confidence,
I find beyond all reasoning.

Though familiar with other performers,
many whose genius astounds,
far from a cause of diversion,
I find Gould's keening profound.
The pianist immersed in the moment,
with rhythms and scales contrapuntal,
I feel him at one with the music,
when he voices a gentle orison,
a tribute made to a great master,
an orphic and deep benediction.

I have heard Perahia's rendition,
his tone mellifluous and warm.
Lang Lang's a performance of genius,
while Frisch finds joy in each theme.
Each brings unique interpretation,
finds colour in each dancing tune,
while remaining verbally silent,

wrapped warmly in Bach's arabesques.
But it is Gould to whom I am ever
returning when drawn to these pieces.

Sing on Glenn Gould, intone softly,
share with us your love for the music.
Sing on Glenn Gould, and show us
how Bach has possessed your soul.

Casablanca Heroes (Play it Sam!)

From that moment she walked into the gin-joint,
it was impossible that any could have told,
how rapidly the fates would conspire,
and the histories of lovers would unfold.
So rarely has a story had two leading men,
seemingly so different in aspect,
the first an archetype all action hero,
while the second shows apparent disconnect.
Victor Laszlo the suave resistance fighter,
has taken arms against the Nazi threat,
while Richard Blaine beneath the shield of Vichy,
decides not to reveal his hand just yet.
Hero one, having cast off prison shackles,
oblivious to what happened there in Paris,
now finds himself beholding to the second,
who holds the key to unlocking his stasis.
Between them stands a woman so divine,
who knows the secret to unite the two,
whose choices will decide the fates of both,
leaving her conflicted and confused.
Ilsa Lund the Swedish beauty so distraught,
calls upon her lover to show pity,
begs him to forgive her for desertion,
when he'd been forced to flee the eternal city.
All this takes place while seated at the piano,
Sam gives voice to a once forbidden song,
wondering what the outcome of events may be,
he expects to see a reckoning before too long.
Not for the first time Rick is called upon,

to make fateful decisions for them both
and gazing into tearful eyes and softening his heart,
he finally comes around to see the truth.
The final scene played out upon the airstrip,
confirms what all along we thought we knew,
that when at last the denouement arrived,
the nightclub owner was a hero too.
A story with two heroes maybe has one flaw,
that no matter how the action may unfurl,
one hero will be left standing in the rain,
because only one can fly off with the girl!
"Here's looking at you kid!"

Lament for Men Who Harvested the Seas

Hardy men their leathered salt burned features,
scowled beneath their worn grease blackened caps,
braced against the swell that kicks and pitches,
and spiteful North Sea winds that roar and slap.
Raging at the fisherman's audacity,
questioning the meaning of his quest,
as he stoops to grip the crystal cutting ropes,
to haul aboard his coble, weed entangled pots.
A lobster man as fine as those who came before,
down many generations, harvesting the seas so vast.
Born into tradition, hewn from long wrought tidal lore,
possessed of learning never taught in class.
A nobleman revered along Northumbrian coasts,
striving still to make an honest living from his boat.

On Keralan beaches wizened men haul lines
hard against the rolling surf that crashes and sucks sand.
Salt beaten men, eyes reddened from the brine,
lean to their labours, heels dug deep into the sloping strand.
Grasping for a rhythm that just might ease them in their task,
each one knows and plays his part rehearsed across the years.
This the destiny they own, no fisherman may flinch or pass,
defeat is not an option, not even as the harsh rope sears.
And as the net draws nearer, with final efforts men defy the waves,
as every man with each yard gained holds firmly to his dream,
to see a greater bounty than he's known for many days,
but fearing that those plenteous times will never more be seen.
Will these men whose ancestors found riches in the sea,
be the first who cannot leave their sons a long-held legacy?

The years when men could rightly talk with pride
of dropping nets or casting lines or heaving pots,
to harvest fish, who knew so well the oceans wide,
could read the currents and the tides, and how to plot
a course to find, the silver shoals that glittered under moonlight.
And danced and dashed before the prow that cut through waves,
as giving chase those hunters of the seas gave all in fight,
against the elements that crushed the will of any but the brave.
Those days and nights that once enabled men who venture to the seas,
returning satisfied to shores well laden with their labours fair reward,
content each time to travel home with catch enough to feed their families,
have long since passed until today not one can ever be assured.
As men who sit in comfort make their fortunes by exploitation of the seas,
and deny their actions, which will see the death of such a fine community.

Eclogue for a Time of Plague

Omnia vincit amor et nos cedamus amori*

Even in a time of cholera love may yet prevail,
or so Marquez would have it, and who am I to doubt?
Fermina and Florentina, true lovers sail on forever,
beneath a yellow flag, from which all others blanch,
and steadfastly maintain an anti-social distance.

Omnia vincit amor

But Marquez created fiction, a fantasy, a fable,
disease in his telling a device to suit his purpose.
A matter of deception to prolong the tryst of lovers,
drawn from the writer's armoury to bring to a denouement,
a tale of love and sorrows demanding bitter-sweet endings.

Omnia vincit amor

Today the plague that haunts comes not from imagination,
reality arrived here with a far more acrid taste.
Each day the numbers rise as horrors that surround us
are growing ever greater, leaving bitterness and tears,
pillaging each nation with a stranglehold of anguish.

Omnia vincit amor

In times of devastation, we must look to the future,
recalling those who outlived such pestilence before.
Defoe who once saw plague that ravaged streets of London,

Boccaccio's Brigata who fled from the black death,
Camus in Algeria where he witnessed early lockdown.

Omnia vincit amor

Such writers conveyed truth and at times saw hope receding,
those witnesses who observed days of sorrow and despair.
But each one understood as they told their tales of tragedy,
that love would gain the upper hand and once again prevail,
as throughout all our history, love has and always will.

Omnia vincit amor
Omnia vincit amor
Omnia vincit amor et nos cedamus amori

* "Love conquers all; let us, too, yield to love!" (Virgil, *The Eclogues*)

Unknown Others

When it comes to matters of identity
of the central figure there is no doubt.
The ashen flesh that clings to bone
and hangs from bloodied sinews wrenched.
The pierced feet, the weighted head,
the token cloth, false shield to modesty.
Stolen, too late, too late as now,
those standing by must testify.
Every stare and knowing gaze,
bears witness that this is the man,
Ecce Homo hoisted high,
victim of man's savagery.

See there, the lady swoons and fades,
caught in the arms of those who feel
that they should share with her the pain,
but know that words afford no ease.
This scene of anguish, bitter grief,
cruel recognition of the truth,
all are helpless, all actions futile.
A bitter moment, time stands still,
naught but emptiness, all is void.
Darkness and tears all that remain.

Regard those others clothed in finery,
mounted on stallions, gilded and groomed.
Expressions indifferent but there to be seen,
part of the crowd, best seats in the house.
Asserting their stations, each holding a pose,

ensuring that theirs will be places in history.
Immortalised characters captured in tempera,
Fra Angelico gifts them a place for eternity.
Fine furs and silks, gilding and tresses,
each one a witness, bit-parts in a drama.

When working his genius and plying his craft
might the artist perhaps have thought, that today
those who stand in awe of his masterpiece
would recall the names of two characters only?
She who distraught lies tended by friends,
and he the victim of barbarous deeds.
While others here featured as part of the scene
have faded from memory, erased over time,
nameless, forgotten, their ambitions thwarted.

A moment in time, portrayed for posterity,
Fra Angelico conveys in his picture a truth,
that most are destined to be side-lined by history,
and that even in this there is a strange irony.
The ones now forgotten when this picture was made,
were there in the flesh in full view of the artist,
while those who today are remembered and named,
were summoned from deep in his imagination.
And so, it would seem even those who are curious,
and wish to know more of the fine clothed strangers,
must content themselves that they will for ever,
remain to be seen as the unknown others.

The Muse

Janey Morris needs no telling.
As she enters the room all heads turn,
conversations falter and women,
each one here, more plain than Jane,
regard their husband's reactions,
and grip their arms to anchor them.
Observe each man and follow his eyes,
and see now how they fail to disguise,
the thoughts that take hold of their minds,
as Jane now holds them captive.
With misty eyes, and pouted lips,
luscious, moist and bidding,
she turns her head, and auburn locks
gently caress her ivory shoulders,
and tumble to stroke her breasts.
So conscious of her audience,
yet she's giving nothing away,
and with this Janey holds the stage,
knowing that this is always the way.
See Dante Gabriel, the favoured one,
all watch now as he approaches.
But even he must surely know,
that Jane bestows no favours,
he too can only gaze and wonder
at the mystique of the muse before him.
Standing alone in the corner,
overlooked by those here assembled,
William watches his wife and smiles.
And when Jane looks up and sees him,
she crosses the room and plants a kiss,
to break the collective reverie.

Sleepless

The ticking of the minute hand my bitter enemy,
harsh rocks where downy pillows should have been.
Each crease beneath my torso turned to ridges magnified,
restless limbs tangled round in strangling sheets.
Too hot this minute, cast off oppressive covers,
no, too cold, reach down draw up the cloth.
Repeat the twist from right to left and back,
draw up knees, stretch out straight, turn over.
These arms, not mine, do not belong,
that cursed ticking clock repeats,
each minute strikes but never moving on.
With each drumming heartbeat's pound,
dancing images, spirits in a restless mind,
dawn no nearer, sleep slips away with hope.
Lethe accepts defeat once more,
condamné à une nuit sans fin.

The Man Who Would be Tsar

The man who would be Tsar
sits at the table alone.
Pig-eyed Billy-No-Mates,
surveying the scene of his works.
Here is the devastation,
here the sour-fruits of his labours.
He casts a long black shadow,
that dooms his people to darkness.
There at the head of the table
surrounded by empty chairs,
the man who would be Tsar
wonders where they have gone,
those who he thought to rule,
those who he felt would bow down.
From a distance they are watching,
what they see is a creature pathetic,
living his self-made nightmare,
deluded, sad and bitter,
like a drunkard lying in the gutter
or a man who knows no poetry.

Carousel Roulette

All too familiar,
that air of resignation,
reality born out of experience.
Half an hour watching cases come and go,
some now on their twentieth lap,
while others snatched eagerly,
never really got to feel the ride.
Numbers soon diminish,
as bags and grateful owners reunite,
the sense of relief palpable.
Can I detect an air of smugness
on the part of the those who now escape,
towards the exit, where awaiting taxis
hurry them to final destinations?
While I am left here filling forms
to confirm once more that I've become,
a loser in this game of baggage lotto.

Monsoon Season, Phnom Penh

Percussive spears of rain bounce high and roll across the red tin-roof,
an urgent parradiddle-rattle opposite the window where I sit.
This in turn is overpowered by the rumbling rage of thunder,
that grumbles angry overhead and shakes the room around me.
Steam billows from the tarmac, whirling upwards on the cloying air,
as limbs of trees convulse and urge away their dripping loads.
Bamboos tick and clatter their convulsive dances in the wind,
while wettened palm barks shine, their lush fronds deluge
weighted.
A heavy purple-mourning sky looms heavy on the city,
where cascades over awnings define safe pedestrian routes.
And in the streets the children carry shoes above their heads
as half-calf deep they rush for home and push against a flowing tide.
Leaf choked drains surrender; their hoped-for task proved helpless,
and women curse umbrellas, so pathetic against the torrent.
Safely seated in this room I shelter and draw breath,
thankful for cooler air I know will follow this savage storm.

Dandi Beach 1930

Twenty days along the road from Sabarmati,
seventy-eight struggled to keep your pace.
Through Nadiad and Kankapura,
Derol, Mangarol and Surat,
tens of thousands cheered and lined the route.
Seventy-eight soon became five hundred,
five hundred then was multiplied tenfold.
Until upon the wave-kissed beach at Dandi
fifty thousand souls had gathered at the shore.

Light glinting from fast in-rushing waters
could never hope to match the spark of fire,
that kindled and ignited in your eyes,
and brought tears to a nation that held breath.
As stooping low to fill your palm with brine,
you raised it high above your head to symbolise,
and show the world how on the beach today you wrote,
the opening of the final chapter of your magnum opus.
By seemingly a simple act committed in defiance,
long passages of pomp and grandeur were disrupted.
And thus, it was that on that day beside the sea at Dandi,
a creaking empire moved towards its death throes,
the one time mighty felled, by a mere handful of salt.

Tamarashasana*

Words etched deep in copper,
afforded greater permanence
than those we trust to paper.
Epigraphy tantalises with summations,
as an all-commanding king demands,
his edict having once been heard
will hold no sway with disputation.
Hear the word of mighty Someshwara
originator and sole arbiter of laws.
His, the only gospel must be heeded,
seek not to question his authority.
Plates of copper stand for ever,
bound and clasped with a tiger's claw.
Centuries have passed since their creation,
note how copperplate inscription
even now, presents the letter of the law.

* The Government Museum in Bengaluru (Bangalore) South
Indian contains a small collection of Indian copper plate inscrip-
tions (tamarashasana), which record the granting of land by
rulers from across several centuries. An impressive example is
that issued by the Hoysala King Someshwara in 1253 AD, which
consists of five sturdy plates bound together with a heavy ring
bearing a seal depicting a large cat (possibly a tiger), that seems
to signify power.

Ramakrishna Temple, Belur, Kolkata

Those who came as pilgrims more focused than the others,
whose innate curiosity simply brought them here to see,
though maybe not to understand the offerings that were made,
by those whose supplications sought Dharma from the gods.

The ornate sacred temple, with nine imposing Navaratna spires,
wherein a marble edifice of Ramakrishna sits cross-legged.
Where many devout faithful had fallen to their knees,
and others looked for blessings prostrate before the figure.

Coolness and tranquillity, rarely found in Indian cities,
but here peace and reverential silence was the order.
Though I came not as a pilgrim, I too could sense the awe and
knew,
the privilege of being with those who understood more than I was
able.

Lindisfarne

The cold sea surrounds
Bitter winds cut from the north
Seagulls dance in clouds.

Above the shingled strand
Castle walls ascend from rocks
Hear the jackdaw's caw.

Paths where pilgrims trod
A thousand years of footprints
Cross the grassy ridges.

Listen to the voices
Carried on the North Sea wind
Echoes across centuries

Tides come in and steal
The only way to mainland
Silence must return.

Hag Stones

Hung from cords on doorposts,
on the glazy flinted cottages
of storm struck Norfolk coasts.
There, my first encounter,
seen but not yet understood.

First along the blasted dunes,
skin-whipping marram
scourging naked shins,
where blue grey holly
and sea-pink edged the path.

Still no relief along the beach
as sand flies spring and irritate.
Until at last where shingle,
sand and pebbles coalesce,
the hunting ground is gained.

There at the meeting point,
where spume and sand converge,
ankles foam washed cold
with the rasping pull of tide,
I turned a thousand salted stones.

They tell me of no need to seek.
That should the stones desire,
and see you as a favoured one,
then they will come to you.
Such is the lore of hag stones.

Late in the day departing the strand,
a canvas bag weighted my shoulder,
concealing a shoreline bounty,
that grated and rattled as I stumbled
across the restless shifting dunes.

I never have believed the myth,
that says that threaded hag stones
hung from eaves, at prows of boats,
or on the stable doorpost,
protect against spirits unseen.

But now within my garden,
neatly assembled hag stones
each conjoined with thread,
bring questions from my friends,
those same that I had asked.

Why here and to what purpose?
And all I can reply, is that
there dwells within us still,
those myths and fables from the past,
and not all actions seek for reason.

The Lost City

Having crossed the wind blessed heath,
and standing at the edge of land,
before me lay a sweep of sand,
and open sea revealing nothing.

Had I not known the history,
and come here as an innocent,
in ignorance of what occurred,
I'd not have stared so long.

The story as I once heard told,
reported storms on two saint's days.
The first swept dwellings to the sea,
the second sounded a death knell.

St Lucia's storm issued a threat,
a harbinger of worse to come,
and then a final coupe de grâce,
brought by St Marcellus' hand.

So little substance can be seen
of a city that had once here stood,
where all that remains as evidence,
are a few Franciscan crumbling walls.

Old wives tell that there are nights,
when sounding out across the waves,
St Katherine's bell is heard to knell,
to mourn the loss of Dunwich.

But looking out at steel grey seas,
today I only trust the words
of those who guard the histories,
of people who once lived here.

As tides assault East Anglian coasts,
I wonder if in future years,
the land on which I stand today,
may have joined the long-lost Dunwich.

The last mermaid has departed from Cathay*,

The last mermaid has departed from Cathay,
and with her demise the romance of sailors has gone.

Those mangroves that afforded shelter,
and soft waving meadows of seagrass,
soon to be erased from memory,
mourned only by old men once beguiled,
and aroused by a vanishing tail.

Seamen from lost generations,
warned of the mystique of sirens,
swore truth in the tales of creatures,
who lured the naïve and the feckless
to shipwreck in a fair mermaid's arms.

It will not be far into the future,
children then will read only of myths,
that enclose those magnificent creatures,
whose gentle passage through shallows,
held past generations in thrall.

The romance of the sailors has gone
with the departure of mermaids from Cathay.

*Researchers have declared a mammal related to the manatee -
said to have inspired ancient tales of mermaids and sirens -
extinct in China.
     BBC News August 24, 2022

Too Little Too Late

Earth crumbles like burnt paper, dust dispersed on wind,
where golden corn should dance in summer breezes.
Withered stalks of ebony, black as rotted teeth,
where sunflowers might have turned their heads
to follow changing hours of the day.
This declared a record year but who would wish to own,
the trophy now awarded for such misery?
A year of children forced to drag their buckets across plains,
where once a mighty river brought some life,
praying that a trickle might tomorrow be a stream.
Fires rage and sear relentless, consuming tinder lands,
outpacing and outwitting all who try to flee its path.
Those whose homes had seemed secure in a canopy of trees,
who have no power to change the ways of avaricious man,
now believe for them that there is neither hope nor future.

Parched earth screams out for want of water
Too little, too little – too late.
Too little – too late
    Too late

A man clings to the rooftop and stares in disbelief,
as the river once so distant now races through his home.
His wife holds fast to children, lest they should all be lost,
one careless slip is all that is required,
to see her precious infants slide away from her to drown.
Scouring the horizon, they can no longer see,
where waving cotton once promised rich harvests.
As trees that had stood proud so long, rush hasty on their way,

dashed against the debris that they had once called village,
beneath the torrent and lost perhaps for always.
Faith long ago departed as the man searches grey skies,
no longer does he believe in salvation.
The promises of those who said they valued every life,
seem empty now and fade with every second,
this no longer is his future; this is the here and now.

A world screams for assistance
Too little, too little – too late.
    Too little – too late
  Too late

Indigenous

Had they waited long to be discovered,
those ancestors from my distant past?
Were their lives obscured by clouds
that fogged their understanding?

I draw upon my learning; all I came to know,
firm foundations built upon the dreamtime.
Our histories, our shared and guarded truths
come down to us from early generations.

My people Ngaanyatjarra, I often see them,
in my lucid dreams asleep and waking.
I see them and listen when they speak to me,
never have they told of days when they were lost.

Discovery, a word with devilish meaning,
slips lightly from tongues of those who would
have us believe, that theirs is a history
with currency far richer than our own.

Are we for ever destined to be grateful,
to those enlightened souls who crossed the oceans?
Brave pioneers Janszoon, Damier, Cooke,
who came to free us from the veil of darkness?

I search my dreams and question those my elders,
whose memories stand firm across all time.
None tell of dark days when they sat and waited,
none can recall a time of being lost.

They tell rather of days when this was our land,
when early people, Ngaanyatjarra, Djaru, Talandiji,
with confidence walked across the rich red soils
that were familiar, not knowing that they waited.

Those who came, they talked of finding new lands,
and having come they claimed them as their own.
While those my elders who had never realised,
their place in life was waiting to be known.

And having been discovered did this set us free?
Did relief come now that we at last were found?
Were we glad to be released from our ignorance,
by civilising hands that sought to raise us up?

Discovery, the term implies new learning,
and with this can come greater understanding.
But only when those who lay claim to what they find,
can recognise that those they found were never truly lost.

Ballad of an Escaped Pig

(Perhaps doggerel, more likely Piggerel!)

Pig was where Pig should not be!
She'd first been seen out on the road,
no respect for the Highway Code.
The driver who she'd caused to stop,
swore that he'd never had a drop.
A pig he cried, a pig for sure!
Maybe a sow, perhaps a boar.
The policeman noted in his book,
and gave the driver a knowing look.
By this time, Pig no longer there
had gone in search of finer fare.
She snuffled her way along the verge,
stopping whenever she felt the urge
to push her snout into the ground,
in hope that bounties may be found.
Then moving on to a new sown field
to see what delights it might yield,
she grunted as she turned each sod
leaving her mark where're she trod.
Earthworms beetles, tender shoots,
lush green leaves and gnarled roots,
each one made a tasty morsel,
as she ploughed on without a scruple.
Crashing through the bramble patch,
oblivious to those thorns that scratch,
She found a pile of sugar beet,
crunchy, succulent and sweet.

Until at last her needs were sated,
she turned for home feeling elated.
But when she returned to her pen,
she could not enter there again.
The hole through which she'd made her exit,
had been discovered and the farmer fixed it.
The escapist pig was no longer bold,
the night was long and dark and cold,
she thought it best to wait around
in hopes that she'd at last be found.
Then we two came upon the scene,
hardly believing what we'd seen.
A Gloucester Old Spot wandering free,
surely not how things should be!
Pig she looked us in the eye,
I need to get back to my sty.
Our porcine knowledge is not great,
how should we now open the gate
to help Pig return to her sty,
and prevent others who might try
to taste the freedom she had found,
and just like her to churn the ground?
With furrowed brows, our heads we scratched,
until at last a plan we hatched.
That gang of pigs, that porky brood,
we knew would be tempted by food.
And so, we searched around until
we found nearby a pail of swill,
and tossed this deep into the sty,
Sara opened the gate while I
pushed Houdini from behind,
encouraging her to go and find
those friends who she had longed to see,

having grown tired of being free.
The gate secured and Pig at home,
we rejoiced at a job well done.
With one last look we checked to see
that Pig was there where Pig should be!

Chance Meeting

(A poem for two voices to be read aloud)
On 10th June 1904 While walking in Nassau Street Dublin,
James Joyce and Nora Barnacle met for the first time.

Nora:
Today, I thought belonged to me,
for a while Finn's can go hang.
Enough of scrubbing tiled floors,
forget the soiled bedsheets.
Today is for a Galway girl
to do just as I will.
An innocent at large (*Ho, Ho*),
to strut the Dublin lanes.
When strolling there down Nassau Street,
a-minding of my own,
I caught first sight of a rolling gait,
perhaps a Swedish mariner
or maybe just a Dub Jackeen.
More likely another chancer.

James:
I saw her from a distance first,
distracted from my reveries.
Shapely, comely, perhaps more.
Nothing better on my mind,
worthy of a closer look.
Looking up I knew that she
had seen that I was watching,
yet not a blush was to be seen,

perhaps I'll chance my arm.
Five yards away I blocked her path,
and tapping lightly my cap's peak
I smiled and nodded just enough,
to show I might have interest
in gaining her acquaintance.

Nora:
Just as I thought a bold young cove.
But now he's caught my eye
he thinks he has the upper hand,
Just see the swagger in the man.
The jaunty cap, says couldn't care,
hands thrust deep in empty pockets.
Who's he kidding, I've got him read,
thinks he's seen an easy win.
Bet he won his spurs with the doxies
down there in Lower Temple Street.
I'll have him know I'm not a girl like that.
Though now he's near I can see,
he has a certain winning smile,
and a shine about his roving eyes.
I'll play this fish until I see
the colour of his gills.

James:
First glance didn't do her fair.
Up close she is a shapely lass.
One might say a fair colleen,
a comely wench with whom I feel,
that should I play a clever hand,
I may find treasures hidden there,
waiting to be unlocked.

Nothing ventured, faint heart,
and all the nonsense rest,
my mind's made up, so here I go.
"Good afternoon miss, (doffing cap)
and a fine one to be sure.
And one that's all the better for
the grace you surely bring,
to lighten up and add new life
to the streets of this fine city."

Nora:
Bold for sure, just as I knew,
he thinks he's got a chance.
I've seen that look of his before,
I know what's on his dirty mind.
Well maybe he will give some sport,
let's see the mettle of the man.
He may be worth more than a glance
but I'll see first how he's made.
"So, is it me you're speaking to?
Do you think perhaps you know me?
Maybe you've mistaken me for
some floosy from your shady past.
If so, I'll bid you get along,
and let me pass, no more ado.
Good day yourself young man."

James:
A maid from the west I do detect,
from Galway I'd place a wager.
A brash response, I like her tone,
a girl who comes on strong.
I like the feisty way she speaks,

no mealy-mouthed replies from her.
I see a challenge in her eyes,
this calls for flattery, I'm sure.
"How could I ever have confused
your grace for that of any other.
Not one from among the very few
with whom I've made acquaintance,
could ever hold a light to you,
whose smile would be sure
to brighten the dull and tired streets
of this city where all else bows,
in acquiescence to your beauty."

Nora:
Well, here's a man with pretty words,
who thinks I'll be won over.
I'll joust with him before I know
whether he's worth the bother.
"Your words are full of flattery,
you spout your pretty phrases,
but I prefer a man of deeds.
I find it's seldom that a lad
who having kissed the Blarney,
can offer more than empty noise
to hold a lady's interest.
So, I ask you kindly step aside
and let me be upon my way,
unless of course you feel sure
that you can give me cause to stay."

James:
A razor tongue to match her looks,
but in her words, I sense

I may have piqued her interest
and given cause to wonder.
Words cannot hide the meaning
I see written on her face,
and see now how she tarries
in hopes I'll take her bait.
"The cause to stay you seek from me
I hope I may provide,
I had a fancy for a stroll
perhaps across of Stephen's Green,
or maybe along Liffey side.
But rather than to walk alone
I'd like to have some company,
and none better than your own."

Nora:
Oh see, I have this fellow hooked,
but I'll put him yet to the test.
If he's to spend some time with me
he'll do so on my terms.
"Young man, I must confess that I
am today bound upon an errand,
but if the words you speak are true
and your gilded tongue sincere,
then I may have space in my diary
to meet with you tomorrow.
Please make yourself presentable
and be sure not to be late,
I suggest that we should meet at noon
outside the Wilde residence,
which you'll find in Merrion Square."

Jim:
Success came here more quickly
than I'd have bargained for.
And now this lass is surely won,
but I'll not be seen as easy.
"I believe that I can find a space
within my busy schedule.
Indeed, for a lady of your bearing,
I'll ensure that I am free.
Number One in Merrion Square
at noon will suit me fine.
But let us not part now without
me knowing of your name,
to all my close acquaintances
I'm simply known as Jim."

Nora:
"Jim let it be then, simple as you say,
at least it's one not easily forgotten.
As for myself my name is one
whose origin they say derives
from honour, I'll have you note.
Gentlemen of limited acquaintance
address me as Miss Barnacle,
those few of whom I may approve,
may come to call me Nora.
But now good sir… or rather Jim,
as you would as soon be called
you have delayed me far too long,
engaged in idle chatter.
For now, I must bid you goodbye.
perhaps to see you later."

Jim:
"Until tomorrow then at noon,
I'll be at Wilde's place.
And hoping for fair weather,
we'll surely take our time,
to get to know each other as
we take the Dublin air.
But now I'll not delay you more,
as you complete your errands.
I'll return home to count the hours,
long and tedious for sure
until mid-day tomorrow."
I sense a future with this lass
may be filled with countless pleasures.
My aim tomorrow will for sure
be to win the heart of Nora.

On June 11th, 1904, James Joyce waited for Nora Barnacle outside Sir William Wilde's house. 1 Merrion Square, but Nora stood him up. James was a persistent man and a few days later, on June 16th, they were finally together, a meeting so significant that it will for ever be remembered through the pages of Ulysses and the annual commemorations of this great novel on Bloomsday, as June 16th has come to be known.

Acknowledgements

Some of the poems in this collection have previously been published elsewhere.

Thurlestone Plovers – in *Poetica Anthology (Volume 9)*
A Man Who Talks to Trees – in *Silence Anthology* (2022)
My Grandfather's Allotment – in *Peeking Cat Literary Anthology 40*
Lament for Men Who Harvested the Seas – in *Taj Mahal Review*
Unknown Others - in *Muddy River Poetry Review*
Final Meeting – in *Hyderabad Literary Festival Magazine, Khabar*
All the Men and Women Merely Players – in *Muddy River Poetry Review*
Say it with Flowers – in *Poetica Anthology (volume 7)*
Casablanca Heroes (Play it Sam) – in *Spillwords Literary Magazine*
Monsoon Season, Phnom Penh – in *Anak Sastra*
Dandi Beach 1930 - in *Hyderabad Literary Festival Magazine Khabar*
Lindisfarne – in *Better than Starbucks*
The Last mermaid has Departed from Cathay, and Too Little Too Late – in the anthology *Dhara – A Paradise Worth Fighting For*

Graham was first read at the memorial service celebrating the life of Graham Matthews, I am indebted to his wife Denise for her consent to reproduce it here in this collection.

Chance Meeting was given its first performance on Bloomsday, June 16th, 2023, beside the grave of Lucia Anna Joyce, James Joyce's daughter who is buried in Kingsthorpe Cemetery,

Northampton. The part of Nora Barnacle was performed by Beverley Webster with Daniel Burrows in the role of James Joyce. Both actors live in Northamptonshire.

The cover image was created by the artist Jean Edwards. More of her work can be seen at https://jeanadrawingaday.com/

I am grateful to the editors of magazines and anthologies who make a commitment to both writers and readers.